CW00431224

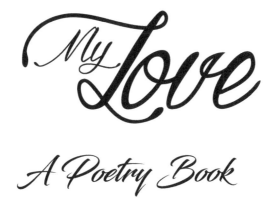

My Love

A Poetry Book

ELIJAH NAPURI

AuthorReputationPress®

Creativity & Branding

Author Reputation Press LLC
45 Dan Road Suite 36
Canton MA 02021
www.authorreputationpress.com
Hotline: 1(800) 220-7660
Fax: 1(855) 752-6001

Ordering Information:
Quantity Sales. Special discounts are available on quantity purchases by corporations, associations, and others. For details, contact the publisher at the address above.

Printed in the United States of America.

ISBN-13   Softcover   978-1-95102-052-1
              Hardcover   978-1-95102-021-7
              eBook   978-1-95102-053-8

To whom ever may stumble upon this book in their journey, I dedicate this to you.

CONTENTS

Our Memories

I can't go on any longer.
The only thing holding us together now, are our memories.

WAITING

Waiting is my specialty you see—I can wait until the end of days.

Until the sun doesn't shine anymore.

Until the universe crashes all around us.

Time would do no such thing for you.

But I will.

Used To

I used to know a man. A man who spoke in soft words and reminisced in memories. A man who'd give his heart and ask for nothing more in return than just your time. A man who used to laugh and love with the fear of losing it all. I used to know that man—and I hope I see him again.

SIGNALS

Frustrations of the game we play. I can't get enough but neither can you. The signals are endless, just like time. And you bombard me with efforts, like the light in the sky. You figured I had brush them off or just hadn't noticed. But baby—I've known all along.

CAN'T

My heart has become too big to fill. I've tasted love and now I am addicted. My heart floods with emotions and my eyes fill with tears. I can't be what you want me to be, but that's okay—because we'll both find our way in the end.

Won't

I want things to happen for us.

I want to see things through with you.

I want to grow together.

I want us to open up and spread our feathers.

I want it all for better or worse.

But it won't be... and it's all because of me.

LOVE

I think Love is like a flower. You pick and give it to someone special. And even though you both may enjoy it for a while, the mere action of you picking it to begin with is what causes its death.

The White Wall

Walking out of the door, I feel my heart drop.

Overwhelmed with emotion and thought.

I can't bare this feeling.

I feel distraught.

Only to turn the corner and see my heart standing there
by the white wall.

Shooting Stars

The night was young and so were we. Staring into her eyes
gave me butterflies because I knew what was on both of our
minds. We looked up at the sky to see shooting stars, and
that was the moment we fell into each other's arms.

CUPID

Feeling numb and undone.

I dreaded this day—the day it becomes nothing.

I knew it were to come.

Now I'm feeling dumb.

Shoot me with an arrow cupid. Make me feel something again.

INSECURITIES

I don't believe she fully loves me.

I do believe it can end at any minute.

My insecurities overcome me, like a tsunami conquers a city.

I feel like I'm drowning.

I feel like I can't breathe.

Waiting for the sea—to come wash over me.

WITHER AWAY

This is what I was afraid of

This is what I knew would happen.

Once you knew you had me in your clutches, once
you knew you found a way to my heart.

You would have nothing more to do—than to just wither away.

BY YOUR SIDE

I can't help the way I feel. I am who I am and there's nothing I can do about it. I know things aren't the easiest with me, but I promise you I try. I can't say it'll all be worth it because I honestly don't know. But I know if you let me—I'll be by your side.

WISH

I wish for the day you wouldn't have to wish anymore.

SUBLIME

I sit hopelessly by the door waiting to hear your footsteps. I climb into bed hoping to feel your body by mine. I walk into a room you've left only to bask in your everlasting scent. I hope you never change a thing. I want to taste you the same just as you were on the first day. But seeing you one last time will forever make me feel—sublime.

PIECES

I pick apart my heart and all I see are pieces. Pieces
of a puzzle, that need to be put away.

I feel so sad.
What a cliche.

We could've been something, but you did this anyway.

I write this to you now—hoping that you'll see it someday.

COMFORT

I always found comfort in resisting. I had this predetermined
notion that if I opened up entirely, she would only grow
sick and tired of me. Little did I know that being so afraid
of losing her is what inevitably pushed her away.

WILLING

I was ready for all your imperfections.
I was ready for the long days and restless nights.
I was ready to be engulfed in your flames.

I was ready for your baggage.
I was ready to be there.
I was ready for the tears.

I was ready for nothing else to matter in the world.
I was ready to crash and burn.

It broke my heart because I was willing.
Only for you to let me down.

HER FACE

I started to see her face everywhere. Even in my dreams. That's how I knew my journey of a broken heart has just begun.

Eleven Days

You took me on this whirlpool of a ride in such a short period of time. It feels like eons have pasted. It's unfortunate that it couldn't last. But I can honestly say that you took my breath away, throughout those eleven days.

SWEET

She tasted so sweet. Every kiss she planted on my lips was like another brush on a canvas of this ever growing painting. She not only wanted to show me affection but she so desperately wanted me to experience it with her. It was beautiful—like tasting a sunset.

SEE YOU TOMORROW

We never wanted to leave each other's sight. Every time we had to part, every time we had to say goodbye, it would take us back to our most inner child like selves, because we never wanted to let go. Even if it was just for a moment. See you tomorrow was something we must always say. That for us, it completed our day.

MRS.

Mrs. was something I'd say when I would get upset,
but it was also something I'd always dream about. We'd
constantly plan our future together, and it looked so bright.
Dedicating my life to her was something I knew was right.
It was as clear as day. Nothing else made sense.

NEGLECT

I've hit a wall in my life.

A hole in the road.

Every day I wake up and tell myself I know what I want and if I just keep holding out and putting off I'll find someone who does as well.

The only problem with that is, I want it so bad that I neglect it.

A classic case some would say.

Elevated

I felt like I could see the path she paved to get to this
perfect place on earths blue sky. I felt elevated. Time is not
a factor for her. It doesn't exist. It's beautiful you see—the
things we take for granted are usually all around us.

Two Times

When I speak your name, all I hear are birds chirping.

I watch you fly.

Fly up above.

You don't even have to try.

It's what you're made of.

Say you love me two times,

Then blink your eyes.

Wherever you look next,

It's me you'll find.

Scared/Stay

The burning rage in my chest is all too familiar. No matter how many times I tell you to go, please understand that I'm just a scared man at the end of his rope. When I scream *leave* at the top of my lungs and push you away—please know I'll drop to my knees, and beg you to stay.

SUNSET

The feeling I had riding in our old jeep that we fixed up one weekend, just to take along the coast, will be with me for as long as I live. The way you smiled at me as the sunset reflected off your sunglasses will be a still picture in my mind, always. I've never seen anything so beautiful before. And I hope I never do again.

Moments

Urging to plan for our future only distracted me from the bigger picture.
And for me that was simply just being in your presence.
Everything seemed like it was made for us and ours for the taking.
But I only wanted you, and the moments we lived in.

Fall

It broke my heart to watch you fall to the ground. I wanted nothing more than to take your pain away. As I lie to you and tell you everything's going to be alright, I can't help but start to weep myself as we both stand there—caught in a blizzard, hanging in each other's arms. For what felt like forever.

COLLIDE

It always dawned on me, the things we used to argue about.
It never made sense to me, the way we used to scream and shout.

I dwell on the thought that we would only ever get upset
because we simply cared for one another. And whenever
we'd collide—I knew it could be the end of us.

Laugh/Cry

I see you from a distance.

There's nothing better than to hear you laugh.

I can only imagine how long it'll last.

I saw the world crash in front of your eyes.

I promise you I'll be there, when you can do nothing more—than cry.

THINK OF ME

I can feel the sand in between my toes. I can hear the
wind whistling in my ears. With my hands on my waist
I stare across the ocean to where the sun meets the water
and I think of you—In hopes that you think of me.

Intimacy

I never want to confuse you. Complicated is my middle name. Please know that it's not you. The last thing I want to do is push you away. But just know that it has to mean something to me—for there to be true intimacy.

Done

Frustrations are a constant company in my life. An unwelcome
but inevitable part of it. Remembering the bedside kisses
and the coffee talks. I think I'm done with it all. I look over
my shoulder to stare into your beautiful brown eyes one last
time, turning off the lights—than shutting the door.

Thrift Store Jacket

We traveled distances together. *Always on the move* she
would say. Exploring the world as we explored each other.
One day we swapped jackets as a token of trust, and to
this day, even though our lives are so far away, we still hold
them close to us. Around her waist was how she
would wear it and she told me that's where it'll always be.
I wonder if I'll ever see that thrift store jacket again.

I Cry Too

I was never one for love at first sight.

But you struck me by surprise like lightning.

Bringing me into your chaotic life, brought balance to mine.

When you left I fell down.

It became so hard for me to keep a smile,

I couldn't help but frown.

I fell so hard in love with you.

If only you knew how much I grew.

I wish you were standing here right now—so I can let you
know that I cry too.

DISAPPOINTMENTS

Some say alone is a bitter thing, but I say it's sweet. There came a time in my life where my heart couldn't take it anymore and the only choice I had was to resign. No need for a pity party, that's not what this poem is about. I'm only trying to say that I'm content about how the way things went, because I realized that this vicious cycle just kept bringing back to the same disappointments.

PIECES II

I longed for your touch.
Just another second of your time, would've been enough.

My chest burning like wildfire.
The way you loved was always something I admired.

Shooting for happiness is what drove us apart.
Our misery was like an unraveling art.

You broke my heart into a million pieces—
But I couldn't be more in love with you.

Keeper

She was a keeper and I knew it.

But at the time I couldn't show it.

As crazy as that sounds, I truly didn't know how.

I was a fool in love.

Some would just call me a fool.

For letting her slip away.

Now every day is a constant reminder, of what could've been, and the price I now pay.

FAVORITE SHOES

I've been on adventures in these things.
Conquered empires in them.

I've walked a thousand miles for you,
And I'd walk a thousand more if you asked me to.

If the world was scarce of food and water, I'd give you
my last meal and bring you something sparkling.

If you were hurt and in the rain I'd pick you up and take your pain.

If you were stranded, barefoot and scared,
I'd give you my favorite shoes and tell you I'm here.

EXPECTING

No matter how upset I've been
I still want to let you in.

Kiss me when you see me,
And tell me you love me when you leave.

I can feel you flow throughout my veins,
Almost like a disease.

I sit waiting by the phone,
Expecting you to come home.

I still want you.
Even when I don't want to.
And I always will.

ALL BLACK

When we were apart hours turned into days.
A never ending prelude.
A complete daze.

When I'd see you in the hallways, my heart would stop.
What I continue to see in your eyes are tear drops.

I knew you were sad when you wore all black.
Desperate for color.
Wanting so bad to go back.

A Poet

Some say it takes a lifetime to become a poet.

I say all it takes is a broken heart.

THE HOUSE

It was like a whole other world having the house to ourselves. Playing and pretending—living in each other's dreams. We were like little bunny rabbits. Except in multiple places.

Signature

I knew you wanted so bad to feel me, and I wanted so bad
to feel you. When I would caress your face, you would lose
control. When I would squeeze your body against mine,
you would moan moan moan moan. Heavily breathing as
the pace gets faster. You clawing my back as I go harder
and harder. I brush my thumbs across your lips as you lick
them. Our bodies moving together in perfect rhythm.
Dripping with sweat, you yell out my name and in
sequence I yell out yours. As we both finish we look in each
other's eyes in a daze, and whisper, *I love you*. You bite my lip
just hard enough to make me bleed, letting me know I'm yours.
Like a signature. I tuck my head in your shoulder, holding
each other close, and there we lay until the sun came up.

Butterfly

What's the butterfly thinking?

It flaps its wings endlessly, with so much hope in its heart.

What's the butterfly thinking?

Its life is so simple yet so precious.

What's the butterfly thinking?

Does it know that it's wild and free?

Breaking from the cocoon and flying away.

I hope I have the courage someday.

LADYBUG

You're so gentle.

So good to me.

So loyal, and so true.

I wish I knew, another ladybug like you.

STICKS & STONES

How can she hurt you like this?

You're a big guy right? You can take it.

Oh how dead wrong you were.

You thought that only sticks and stones could break your bones?

She'd spit out lava.

I've never been so hurt by words.

Was I naïve?

How could I have not seen this coming?

It's too late now.

What's done is done.

She'll always be a memory of mine.

The woman with the sharp tongue.

EAST VILLA ST.

Whenever I'm here, I feel shell shock.

Things to remind me of her, up and down the block.

It feels like walking through a snow storm without a winter coat, or swimming in a sea of sharks.

This is where we'd have our long talks and where we always used to meet.

So much has happened to us, on east villa street.

Friend/Family

You said that I didn't fight hard enough.

That I didn't really love you.

I'll always say the same thing, just let me show you.

We had a life together.

Days upon days with each other.

You were my friend.

My family.

My weakness.

My reason to transcend.

I'll always fight for you, until the bitter end.

M&N

They were perfect in my eyes, that's something
I admired about them.

Rarely hearing about bad times, or arguments.

The future looked bright for these two love birds.

Their strive against time was something unheard.

When they fell apart it broke my heart, knowing all the sacrifice.

M & N were their initials.

The only thing missing was forever.

After All

After all, you're not going to get out of this alive,
so why not fail at something you love.

Mini Coopers

I see them everywhere now, it never seems to disappoint.

And I'm not just being nostalgic, although we did have a
connection—so I thought.

Every direction I look there's one waiting for me.

Ridiculous I know, but ridiculous is right.

I feel like one is going to roll up beside me and scoop me up.

Mini coopers just suck.

Reach for Me

Reach for me, I promise I'll catch you.

Reach for me, I promise I'll hold you.

Reach for me, I promise I care.

Reach for me, for I am always there.

Reach for me, I'll be waiting for you.

Reach for me, I'll never let go.

Reach for the moon as I reach for the sun.

Reach for me, until the two become one.

POINT OF VIEW

It's like standing on the sand as the ocean tide comes in
and you feel the sand disintegrate beneath your feet.
That's how it felt from my point of view. That's how it felt
sitting in a room with you. When you were there you
weren't there, even when I wanted you to.

FLOWER

This flower has closed its pedals for the night, waiting for
the sun to arise.

Accept

Our story had ended so abruptly. It's not something you can prepare for, and I didn't know how to take it. Cutting things off cold turkey has always been the easiest for me. I was selfish in that way, and for that I'm sorry.

I looked for you until I was ready to accept that you weren't coming back. It's funny how our hearts work like that.

Beautiful Noise

All our years together and we're still able to make
each other laugh.

Butterflies in my stomach whenever you pass,
and I feel them throughout.

That's how you make me feel baby—everyday,
and without a doubt.

We started something larger than us and now
it has taken control.

Sitting at the dinner table, overwhelmed by all
the beautiful noise.

It's like no other—It's truly surreal.

Just like the day we met, and how you continue
to make me feel.

WOMANIZER

Confusing times and late nights aren't something that mix.

Wanting another for lust isn't something you do for kicks.

A fresh heart looking for love is something
easily misunderstood.

Don't speak to another fresh heart unless you're
staying for good.

Only wanting to talk and just be friends—

The deception of the womanizer is something
that never ends.

CRUNCH

We would hold hands and go for our weekly walks.
We'd stumble upon things like squirrels, bugs, birds, and even lizards.
But there was always something special about leaves. She told me that
when she was younger, she used to think that every leaf she stepped
on was another problem solved. Almost like a wish, but better because
there were plenty to go around. It's like they're infinite. She would do it
relentlessly while holding my hand, and egging me on to do it with her.
We would jump for hours, through so many blocks and I would fall
more and more in love with her along the way. One day she told me
you know there's another reason why I like to step on them, I asked with
fascination; *Why?* She came closer to me and whispered, *I like the crunch.*

GREY

Hold me close as the leaves change color.

Look into my eyes until you see the universe.
Bathing in your words puts me at ease.

I'll be anywhere you want me to be,

Just come and find me.

I live for the good and I live for the bad.

I'll love for the grey and I'll cry for the sad.

Day by day is our only way,

All you need to say is yes.

IF

If love had a sound, it would be your voice.

If love was a decision, you would be the only choice.

If love was a race, you would be first place.

If love was a letter, than it would be K.

If love was a bird, you'd be a blue jay.

If love was in the air, I would inhale without a care.

If love was an animal, you'd never be tamed.

If love was no more, than I'd be the same.

Forever

When I wake, I take a deep breath.

A breath to embrace.

Embrace all your love.

Love that you gave.

Given but not earned.

Earning comes with intent.

Intent to keep it all.

All is more than I deserve.

You deserve better.

Better than me.

Me and you forever, is what I wish we could be.

KNOWING

I'm so in love with you,

It's almost like you cast a spell.

I get so nervous around you,

I pray and hope you couldn't tell.

When you disappeared out of nowhere,

I found myself gasping for air.

Denying is what I did best and it's what I continue to do.

Although this were to come,

It's something that I always knew.

Suddenly I felt melancholy.

I suppose knowing was the cause.

EARTHQUAKE

It was something like a bomb that hit my room. I've never
been so conflicted in my life. With you crying on your
knees and me holding you by your side—I didn't know
whether to be strong or cry. If we were breaking up or
trying again, I didn't know how to feel or what would be
best in the end. All I knew was I was scared. Scared of
losing you. And that I was sorry. Sorry for all I put you
through. As we both get up and hold each other tight, we
agree to choose love, and call it a night. Until
the next earthquake were to arise.

SUBPAR MEMORY

It all happened so fast.
A decision made under the influence,
Or at least I'd like to think so.
We started to undress each other.
It felt so bizarre.
Almost like a cry for help.
A desperate act.

We suddenly stop because I can't follow through.
My nose flares up because my heart's broken too.

It could've gone plenty of ways and I'll think
of them until the end of my days.
Another subpar memory.

Nose Bleeds

I can feel you running down my lips.

An unappreciated gesture.

I hate you at times,

But I know you're coming from a place of love.

The nose bleeds you give me are by far the worst thing
I could receive.

But I never want you to stop.

Out Loud

Her name out loud still gives me goosebumps.

I tremble to the thought of her with another.

It hurt so good when I think of the time shared,

And it hurt so bad when I knew she didn't care.

If only I'd know sooner; would be appropriate to say.

We met when we were young and now I'm in my middle age.

Sad but not sorry, was how I knew she felt.

I suppose that's what you get when something's destine to melt.

Stars

The beautiful thing is, you can see the stars from anywhere. All you have to do is look up.

LAST NIGHT

I didn't know a person like this existed. We became so intimate so fast I didn't know how to take it. Everything felt so real like I've known this person forever, when really she was a complete stranger. I've only ever wanted to make love to a person I'm in love with, but last night showed me different. She became a lover of mine right then and there, and before that I thought you couldn't share such a thing unless you were absolutely in love. It was a puzzling experience. It was an enlightening experience.

ALIVE

Have you ever experienced being in the same room with
someone who you loved and had a life with, only to know
that it's all coming to an end? You both always knew deep down that
it was over but you loved each other too much to let it go. You hold
each other until the morning, dreading to hear the birds chirping
because you know in the morning things will be different. And
it's not so much the breaking up that scares you, but the change
that comes along with it. You built a life with and around this
person you once loved but now—lost. That's the kind of story mine
ended up being. But let me tell you—I've never felt more alive.

LIFE IS STRANGE

Life is too big for labels.

Life is too big to fear.

Life is like a box of chocolates.

Life will always bring you tears.

Life is full of love,

And all its heartbreaks.

In life you'll make love,

But also make mistakes.

Life is too short not to live,

And too long to be sad.

In life you'll make mistakes,

But be glad that you had.

Life is a roller coaster that never ends,

With emotions flying constantly.

Some say life is strange,

But I say it's supposed to be.

SOMEDAY

I saw you in the distance, it felt like any other day.
We were walking across an open grass field, which felt like
it went for miles in every direction. You were wearing a white
silk dress with a very elaborate pattern of golden dragons all over it.
You had on gold lipstick to match the dragons. Your hair up in a tight
bun like how you'd usually wear it, but this time you had these two
thin stands of hair fall on each side of your face like sideburns. You
looked so beautiful. With us both being barefoot I felt the grass
brush across the bottom of my feet with every step I took. It felt like
we were walking under water. As we got closer and closer I began
to smile, and so did you, like we couldn't wait to be in each other's
arms. And then suddenly—you fell to the ground in the blink of an
eye. I rushed to you with my heart racing. Sliding to my knees as
I looked over your body. I lift your head slowly, tucking it in
my shoulder as I put my hand on your heart. I felt no beat and
I burst into tears. Denying that this could be real; My mind
quickly races with thoughts of the life we would've lived. My head
felt like it was going to catch fire, as so did my chest. I look to
the sky to find answers as I softly sob over and over, asking the
question why? And that's when I burst awake. Hyperventilating
and dripping with sweat I was overwhelmed with relief when I
realized it was only a dream. I know you're out there, and I hope to
live long enough to meet you, and tell you this story someday.

AGAIN

What is love if not sad?

How can we learn to get up without falling to the ground?

I was in love once and it was great, but some days I wish I had met you later in my life. I would've kept my heart whole just for you. You would've been my first for the rest of my life, and every morning I wake it would feel like the first time all over again.

Happier

She told me I was beautiful and that she couldn't be happier.

I couldn't help but hurt knowing I didn't feel the same.

I looked away in shame.

I wanted to believe everything was okay, and I know she did too.

I looked back at her to find that she was crying.

We stared at each other for a few moments,

And then she gave me a nod, letting me know she understood.

She grabbed my hand and there we sat, until it was time to let go.

BEST FRIEND

You were my best friend.

My hero.

I can tell you anything,

And the world would never know.

We can fly high and sore from place to place.

There was never a dull moment.

You would follow me to outer space.

I could laugh and cry and you'd be by my side.

I felt so safe,

Even when I wanted to die.

You liked the things I liked,

Although we'd have disagreements.

I wouldn't trade you for the world,

Even for the world itself.

Slow Mornings

We'd stay up all night and in the morning become
something like zombies. As I wake, I turn to you to say
good morning beautiful, As I brush your golden brown
hair over your ear. You look into my eyes and say
good morning baby, as you peck the tip of my nose
with a gentle kiss. We then began to progress from that
kiss as I come in for another. Your soft moans only make me
want you more. We caress our bodies together and start
to make love. Simultaneously we can hear the birds
chirping outside the window. It was heavenly. Something
out of a book. Another one of our slow mornings.

LITTLE LADY

It was something I'd call you when I was upset.

It was something I'd call you out of love.

My little lady—sent from up above.

You were it.

Nothing can compare.

You were the balance to my counter.

The thing that made me whole.

In you I saw a future like no other,

A place I couldn't wait to arrive.

In you I saw children,

And in them I saw your eyes.

My darling I can't wait to someday look back at our archives.

What a beautiful sentiment that would be.

NAMES

The names we called each other were endless.

Baby was the one we used the most.

I can still hear your voice now.

So vibrant and so beautiful.

It has its own beat.

It's a song to me.

Baby, baby.

You used to make me feel complete.

Winter Rain

I remember the day we had our first argument. We were in high school and it was the middle of winter. You told me you couldn't sleep and that you stood up all night waiting by your phone, hoping I would call. It bothered you to the bitter end and you told me you didn't fully understand why. You said to me it was because you loved me and of course that had to be the only reason why. But you knew there was something else, and you couldn't quite put your finger on it. The day goes on and we meet up by the school gate like we usually do. You tell me that even though it would've only been over the phone, the fact that we didn't say *I love you* to one another took a toll like no other. But you go on to tell me that it was also the fact of us being angry with each other. You told me that you didn't even like the idea of anger standing between us, because you knew our love was much more and that it wasn't worth jeopardizing. I was speechless. I thought that was so beautiful. We kissed and held each other in the winter rain for a while and then kissed one more time. After that we started our walk back home together.

ALGEBRA

We would dance all night.
Your body against mine.
It was a reflection of our love.

We would do long division,
And solve equations.
I've never had a better partner.

You were the answer to my problem.
The missing puzzle.
You turned me into a masterpiece.

Of all the mathematics in the world,
I loved you the most.
My sweet algebra.

BITTER SWEET

We would do it for the thrill.

It was as if we had no other care in the world.

Like the world was built just for us.

You were wild and free,

And in every way you pushed me to be somebody better.

I can never thank you enough.

You would stick by my side,

Even when times would get rough.

We would walk and talk and sit under trees.

We'd run through flower fields, annoying all the bees.

We would laugh and dance and stay up all night.

I loved the nights when we'd hold each other tight.

When you passed away I felt the true meaning of pain.

I sat under our favorite tree, even in the pouring rain.

As I end this poem now and put it to sleep,

I knew at the end—

It would be bitter sweet.

HISTORY

You told me when I held you, your knees felt weak.

You told me when I looked at you, your heart would pound.

You told me when you'd hear my voice, you'd
get butterflies in your stomach.

You gave me a bracelet as a token of your love.

You said you made it when you were sure I was the one.

I told you when I first saw you, I knew I loved you right away.

I told you I saw a future with you, and that it was brighter than the day.

I gave you a necklace as a token of my love.

I told you that you were special and I wanted you
to know that every time you wore it.

And then one day you broke it.

The rest is history.

Love Once Again

A hole in my chest where my heart used to be.

I sit and write this to you hoping you'll see.

I cannot take the stress of this heartbreak.

I'm a total mess and I ache, and ache, and ache.

Unable to stand on my own two feet,

I'll reach for your hand until we finally meet.

It hurts throughout my whole body and x's that by ten.

I know I'll feel this way,

Until I'm ready to love once again.

STILL

I woke up ill.

I recollect from the nightmare I had the night before.

It's hard to breath in the cold of the morning.

I shut my window to catch my breath and see you on the other side.

I wave in expectance but realize it's only a shadow.

I don't know where you've gone, but I hope you're not long.

A hint of sadness then creeped over me just as the sun came up.

It was like we were insync.

If you were a train of thought you'd be the way I think.

Forever and ever like we always used to say—maybe in

the next life I suppose.

For now I remain still.

FRESH AIR

We used to ride bikes in the summer,

Letting go of problems and letting down our hair.

Inhaling you was like a breath of fresh air.

Tears of Joy

I remember us fighting. I remember it getting out of hand.
I never understood why we'd get how we got when we'd argue.
You spend your life thinking you're better than something but
realize you're no better than anybody else. It's a rude awakening,
but a necessary one. I always felt like I had only myself to blame.

I also remember us laughing. I remember it being hilarious.
You always had the best sense of humor. I can practically say
anything. In those moments I thought we were meant to be
because of how good we were together. Every day felt new with
you (in a sense) and every day with you I felt immense.

But you were just a girl and I was just a boy. I suppose the
best way to put it would be, you brought me tears of joy.

INSEPARABLE

I was reminiscing on the story behind the day we met.
From the first time I saw you I knew I had to have you.
I thought to myself *she had to be the prettiest girl I've seen at
this high school*. I was fourteen years old and we were freshmen.
One day you caught me looking your way in class, so I scrambled
to look away in a hurry. I was so embarrassed. I thought I had
blew it. When lunch came around I walked to cafeteria and saw
you sitting by yourself. It was as if you were lighting up the whole
room and everything around you became a distant shadow.
With me thinking what are the odds? I quickly walked over
to introduce myself. I remember it going a little like this:

Me: Hi, I'm anxiety

You: Hi, I'm understanding

We became good friends and quickly became lovers.
We were like two peas in a pod. Like two birds of a feather.
We were inseparable after that.

EXISTENCE

I'm looking at the horizon,

The clouds look like explosions in the distance.

Every day I often wonder if you're aware of my existence.

STRAWBERRY TART

You picked me from a fresh batch of fruit like you were
just strolling on through.

It felt like any ol' day for you.

You held me like a baby, and we became best of friends.

You told me I was your favorite and that I always will be.

You rubbed me, washed me, and loved me.

I felt safe.

Like no other can take my place.

When age caught up with me, you can tell in my face.

It was like you didn't know that age existed.

You seemed to be in denial.

When I went sour, so did you.

I didn't know what to do.

Spending time with you seemed to hurt.

But I won't deny how I feel.

Baby, you'll always have a piece of my heart.

When you finally left—you took a bite out of my strawberry tart.

Cherry Boy/Collapse

They used to call me cherry boy, because
I was more sensitive than others.

I was so insecure at the time, I felt I had to plunder.

You saw me for who I am and not what I was portrayed under.

When I was with you, I didn't need to run for cover.

You were my lover.

From the moon and back until we collapse into one another.

STONES & ROSES

It's funny you see,

When I look back at it now,

It all makes sense to me.

But in the moment I'm blind.

I stand too close to the elephant at times.

When I think of blue, I think of you.

When I think of red, I think of us too.

We've had countless endeavors.

But it wasn't enough.

As this chapter closes,

I'll leave it by saying,

Our relationship was like stones and roses.

Long Term

You never forget your first love.

They become an unforeseen long term.

PINKY PROMISE

We were teenagers in love but nothing else mattered.
The things we would plan were so far away but
we were so eager to live it someday.

I told you I wanted to travel the world and take you with me.
We'd have new experiences and see different countries.
It would be a dream come true and that
I only wanted to do it with you.

You said that you wanted to be an artist and have your own
gallery. Somewhere nice and cheap. But you needed me there
every night laying with you, to be able to fall asleep.

I told you that you can have anything you want.
I'd make enough money to support us two.

You whispered to me, *please promise me that we'll see
these things through*

I whispered back, *pinky promise me that you won't
break my heart.*

You replied, *never.*

You X's Three

If you were here standing right in front of me, the only thing I'd truly be able to tell you is that I missed you.

LOVE ME BACK

I've seen two hearts split in half

I've seen two hearts separate.

I've seen people scream and shout and,
I've seen people laugh and giggle.

I've heard them say with tears in their eyes *love me back* and
I've heard them say with open arms *I love you, relax.*

It's hard to paint a masterpiece.

It's even harder to watch it fall apart.

The following poem was something I wrote to my first love
when I was a senior in high school. I've never written a
poem before this and it took me a while to find the right words.
I kept erasing and rewriting for hours because of how worried
I was of her not liking it until I finally said the hell with it.
I knew if I liked what I wrote and stood by it, she would like it too.
I gave it to her the following day and she loved it. I dedicate this to her.

My Love

My love, where to start.

We've been through so much, it's almost like an art.

I could never break away from you even if I wanted to.

It's a blessing and a curse how much I love you.

But it takes courage to do what we do.

I know I'm not perfect but truth is neither are you.

But I know what we have is more than true.

So much so that we stick together like glue.

You're the only person I'd go miles for,

Even if I had to go to war.

You drive me crazy in such a way,

I don't want to hear half the things you say,

But I know at the end of the day, I love you.

And if I could have anybody else I would always choose you.

I look back and laugh at our past,

Because I knew in my heart that we'd last.

I remember how foolish I was back then.

Hoping it'd get better and ask when.

But looking back at it all now,

I'd do it all again.

January 13th, 2015

ABOUT THE AUTHOR

I grew up in two cities, one was Baldwin Park, California and the other was Pasadena, California. I got very familiar with both cities because my parents never got married and split up just when I was born, so naturally I had to bounce back and forth between the two. I didn't have a terrible childhood but just like any other lower middle class kid, I constantly wished and dreamed of something better. That's where my writing came into play. Although I never had any kind of aspirations of being a writer when I was younger, I always used to notice that it came so naturally. I've always felt like I had a head full of ideas and a heart full of emotions, and if I didn't get them out somehow I was going to lose them, so I had to do something about it. I had no idea coming into this that something so simple and essential like a pen and paper can mean so much. But I'm glad I found it and I'm glad it found me and that's something I intend on forever keeping.

Photograph by Jonathan Garay

CPSIA information can be obtained
at www.ICGtesting.com
Printed in the USA
BVHW071429080819
555426BV00001B/6/P